Community, Culture, and Me

Written by Gavin Worthy

What Is Culture?

KidHaven PUBLISHING

Published in 2027 by
KidHaven Publishing, an Imprint of Greenhaven Publishing, LLC
2544 Clinton St., Buffalo, NY 14224

Written by: Gavin Worthy
Edited by: Doug Barone
Designed by: Ker Ker Lee

Cataloging-in-Publication Data

Names: Worthy, Gavin.
Title: What is culture? / Gavin Worthy.
Description: Buffalo, NY : KidHaven Publishing, 2027. | Series: Community, culture, and me | Includes glossary and index.
Identifiers: ISBN 9781534570016 (pbk.) | ISBN 9781534570023 (library bound) | ISBN 9781534570030 (ebook)
Subjects: LCSH: Culture--Juvenile literature.
Classification: LCC GN357.W678 2027 | DDC 306--dc23

Printed in China

CPSIA compliance information: Batch #QS27KH: For further information contact Greenhaven Publishing LLC at 1-844-317-7404.

Please visit our website, www.greenhavenpublishing.com.
For a free color catalog of all our high-quality books, call toll free 1-844-317-7404 or fax 1-844-317-7405.

Find us on

Photo Credits – Images courtesy of Shutterstock.com, unless otherwise stated.

Cover & Recurring – Dedraw Studio, TVhappyLine, JLco Julia Amaral, Shuttercountproduction. 2–3 – PeopleImages. 4–5 – Rawpixel.com, Monkey Business Images. 6–7 – ivan_kislitsin, Tutti Frutti. 8–9 – Sam the Leigh, MVolodymyr. 10–11 – Anuragfotoz, B Hanson. 12–13 – 2p2play, Mihai_Andritoiu. 14–15 – TeamWajiography, Sun_Shine. 16–17 – fotopanorama360, Wangkun Jia. 18–19 – Maarten Zeehandelaar, Victor Velter. 20–21 – Drazen Zigic, Artush. 22–23 – BGStock72, Graeme J Baty.

Contents

Words that look like **this** can be found in the glossary on page 24.

How We Live

A culture is all the different things that make up how a group of people live. Your culture is part of what makes you who you are.

Different groups of people around the world have their own cultures. Even groups of people from the same country can have different cultures.

The ways you eat, dress, and have fun are all part of your culture.

Food

Food can be a very important part of someone's culture. Eating with others is a way to **bond** and share. Even the ways food is made and cooked are part of cultures.

Many people eat pasta in Italy. There are lots of different pasta shapes.

In southern China, rice is a big part of people's diet. There are lots of rice farms, where people help each other grow enough of this crop. Helping others is also part of Chinese culture.

These are rice farms in southern China.

Music

A culture's music can be modern or traditional. In South Korea, there is a popular type of music today called K-pop. Music videos and dance routines are a big part of K-pop.

a K-pop group on stage

Some music is very important to a group, even if people don't listen to it every day. Traditional Irish folk music is a big part of the history and culture of people from Ireland.

Irish folk music is still played today.

Violins, guitars, harps, and flutes are some of the instruments used in Irish folk music.

Holidays and Festivals

In many cultures, there are special days that everyone can celebrate together. These are called holidays or festivals. Holi is a Hindu festival in India. It is called the Festival of Colors.

Everybody throws colored water and powder onto each other during Holi.

People in Mexico and other parts of the Americas celebrate Día de los Muertos—also called Day of the Dead. This is a day to think about and respect people who have died.

Some people wear wooden masks or paint their faces.

Some families build ofrendas, with candles, photos, flowers, and food.

Religion

Following a religion means believing in a god or many gods. It usually involves behaving in certain ways and following special rules. Religion is a big part of many cultures across the world.

Buddhism is the biggest religion in Thailand. Some Buddhists wear orange robes.

The main religion in Egypt is Islam. Many followers of Islam, who are called Muslims, dress in certain ways and don't eat certain foods. Friday is a day for prayers.

There are many mosques in Egypt, which are special buildings for prayer in Islam.

Clothing

The clothes of a culture can be decided by the weather and materials found in a place. A kilt is a traditional piece of clothing that men wear in Scotland. It is worn at special times.

In Saudi Arabia, light, loose clothes are often worn. This is because it can be very hot there. The clothes cover most of the skin. This is partly for religious reasons.

Religion is very important in Saudi Arabian culture.

How Things Are Built

Buildings and streets can say a lot about a culture. In Copenhagen, there are special bike lanes and lots of space for bicycles. Cycling is popular in Copenhagen and is a big part of the culture.

Copenhagen is the capital city of Denmark.

Japan has many earthquakes. This is one of the reasons why old Japanese buildings were made of wood instead of stone. Wooden buildings were more flexible and could be rebuilt quickly.

Horyu-ji Temple is the oldest wooden building in the world.

Modern buildings in Japan have special ways to deal with earthquakes.

Sports

Some cultures have certain sports that are very important to many people. Soccer is a very popular sport in Brazil. It is played on the streets and beaches, as well as in huge stadiums.

In New Zealand, rugby is a very popular sport. The New Zealand rugby team is called the All Blacks. Before each game, they perform a haka, which is a traditional Māori war dance.

The Māori people were the first people to live in New Zealand.

the haka

What Is Important to a Culture?

Another part of a culture is how people think and what ideas they care about the most. In the United States, many people care about the idea of freedom of speech.

Freedom of speech is the idea that people should be free to express themselves.

Family is important in Ethiopian culture. Many people believe in caring for family members. In many homes in Ethiopia, many family members live together. This includes grandparents, children, aunts, and uncles.

Different but Together

Now you know more about what makes up a culture. There are many cultures around the world, and each one is different. What is important in your culture?

In many places in the world, cultures come together and live side-by-side. Sharing and understanding each other's cultures can make life more interesting. What do you find most interesting about other cultures?

Learning about other cultures can help us build stronger communities.

Glossary

bond	to form a relationship based on love, friendship or loyalty
diet	the kinds of food that a person or group usually eats
earthquakes	sudden, powerful shakes in the ground that can be dangerous and cause damage
express	show feelings and emotions
flexible	having the ability to bend and stretch
modern	to do with recent or present times
ofrendas	places in homes that are decorated to honor loved ones who have passed away
prayers	ways of speaking to a god or gods, to say thanks or to ask for help
respect	honor someone or something
traditional	to do with beliefs, customs, or ways of behaving that have been around for a long time

Index